Primarily Poetry

Poetry Lessons for K-3

Written by **Dr. Lani Steele**
Under the auspices of
the Poets in the School
Illustrated by **Jean Thornley**

Contents

Introduction

About This Book

The lessons in **Primarily Poetry** are drawn from poet-teachers who work with *California Poets in the Schools* (CPITS), a group of published, professional writers who work with children in schools all over the state of California. Recently commended by the California State Legislature, CPITS employs a hands-on approach in which poets share with children their joy of language and some very specific ways to begin writing poetry. The lessons in this book are designed to help teachers recreate the excitement and pleasure in writing poetry that we poet-teachers have experienced in classrooms.

The Basic Model

The basic model for lessons in this book is to present an idea on which poems will be based. Poems are often included to exemplify some parts of the ideas being examined or to help students focus their attention on a particular area. Students are often given a language exercise that isolates the skill or technique that will be used in the poems. Sometimes sample poems provide an exact model. When all ideas and techniques to be included in the poem have been discussed, the teacher leads the group in writing a class poem. For very young students, this is the final activity. For those who can write, the group poem serves as a model. Students then write their poems either individually or in cooperative learning groups. Poems are usually read aloud, either by the teacher or the student poets. It is very important that teachers be willing to read all student poems, anonymously if necessary. This builds student confidence and encourages further writing.

The lessons in this book are presented in such a way that skills are developed in the earlier lessons that can be used in later lessons. The lessons in the beginning of the book also present a structured format, where later lessons are unstructured, allowing for more freedom of expression. When working with students who are new to poetry writing, you should probably use some of the more structured formats to begin. As students become more confident and skilled, they will be able to easily write poems without specific directions as to format.

Poetic Techniques

Although specific poetic techniques are identified at the beginning of each lesson, the main technique that is being developed with these lessons is the expansion of children's imaginations. You will see *use of the senses* many times at the top of the lessons. This may seem repetitious, but the application of this skill grows ever more sophisticated and is always one of the poet's basic tools. Other techniques that are presented are voice (who is talking in the poem), simile and metaphor, language poetry (deconstruction), as well as cross-curricular and multi-cultural techniques. What we want to develop is the students' freedom and boldness in playing with language to express her/himself freely and in an original way.

The overall goal of **Primarily Poetry** is each student's admiration for, comfort and familiarity with, and friendly mastery of some basic tools of language, specifically poetic language. These tools are transferable to any form of writing that requires cogency, wit, and clarity. We hope that students develop an open-minded appreciation of the many ways of writing poetry and an appreciative ear for the poetry of others. We hope that students will see poetry as one way of lighting up the commonplace as well as exalting the extraordinary.

Cooperation

When writing a poem with a large group (either as a sample poem or as a final poem for non-writing students), try to solicit lines from various individuals, or better yet, from groups who collaborate to produce a line. If students are seated at tables, have each table group be responsible for a line. This is a valuable form of cooperative learning, and it helps shyer students become involved.

With students who are just starting to write, group poems, rather than individual efforts, are often a more effective form of writing. Designate functions for the members of the group — the scribe (someone who can write) the monitor (someone who can keep the group on task and quiet), the reader (someone to read the poem aloud), and the encourager. The more practice students have working in groups, the better they will become.

On Your Own

In working with the lessons in this book, please read them over well before beginning. Add anything that will make the lesson more relevant and, thus, more compelling to your students. As with everything else we do, the effect of these lessons will increase by what you personally put into them. If you have favorite poems, use them with a lesson whenever possible. Write with your students when they are writing. Read your own poems aloud to your students.

As poet teachers, we in CPITS have left classrooms with many good poems by our student poets, but more importantly, we have participated in a process that has brought joy to students and teachers alike. We hope that by using these lessons that you will share that joy.

Introductory Ideas and Activities

Suggested by: Jorge Luhan, Carol Lee Sanchez, Lani Steele, John Oliver Simon

Thinking About Children and Poetry

Children know poetry. They are closer to it than adults are. They will tell it to us when they trust us.

Getting Ready for Poetry

1. The poetic chant.

   > *By the mane of the lion,*
   > *By the stripes of the zebra,*
   > *By the fleas on my dog,*
   > *Who wrapped up the elephant?*

   Act out this chant with as much exaggeration as possible. Have students act out the chant with you. Do several times to get students relaxed. Have students make up their own chants.

2. If students are very restless, try this idea:

   Pick out a topic that is related to what is happening in the classroom at the moment. For instance, "How did you feel about coming in from P.E. to do poetry?" Have all students shout together words to express their feelings. Then have all students whisper good, positive words about the topic. Then start your lesson.

3. Read and show students the following "crazy line" poem. Discuss the fact that this is a poem. Poems can be written any way the poet wants. Unlike regular prose, they are not written in sentences and paragraphs.

   > Am i
   > a poem?
   >   WHO says?
   > I do
   > I do
   > I do.

4. Ask students if they are poets. Tell them you will use your magic wand to turn them into poets and release all of their poetic, creative abilities. Wave wand and say anything that sounds like magic words.

Features of Modern Poetry

1. Poet-teachers consistently stress that students **not** write rhyming poetry. Since about 1920 the prevailing mode has been free verse. But the most important reason for not rhyming is that children will warp the sense and meaning of their poems just to get a rhyme. It is preferable that young children work with other poetic techniques that will allow them to express their ideas freely and naturally.

2. The building blocks of poetry are lines, arranged traditionally in stanzas or in any way the poet wishes, including shape poems. Students need to be assured that they **need not**, and indeed should not, write in sentences or paragraphs. Similarly, punctuation and capitalization are up to the poet in free verse. You can point out, however, that in other forms of poetry, more formal rules about punctuation apply.

3. Students should not try to use a regular metered rhythm (ta TUM ta TUM ta TUM, etc.). Cadence may be built up by the placement of words and lines. Sometimes, as in haiku, syllable count makes for some regularity.

4. Usually language in poetry is less formal. Poems can include slang, and, in fact, slang can make the poems vital and immediate.

Introductory Ideas and Activities, continued

Reading

1. Read poetry to students as often as possible. Use a variety of poets and types of poetry. See the bibliography for suggestions.

2. For older students, read a little each day from a long poem such as "Hiawatha" or "The Highwayman."

3. Let students read poems aloud; either their own poems, those of other students, or from favorite collections.

4. Find poems from other cultures to share with students.

5. If there are different voices in a poem (more than one person speaking in the poem), let students read parts as in a play.

Ideas for Lessons

1. Give students a cartoon drawing with no words on it. Let them make up words for the cartoon. Use these words and the situation depicted in the cartoon as a basis for a poem.

2. Show students a favorite painting quickly and then put the picture away. Ask students to describe what they saw. Elicit as many responses and different ideas as possible. Get the story of the painting and/or the images, then have students write a poem about the painting.

3. Students in third grade should be able, with practice, to translate poetry into prose and vice versa. Read a poem, have students paraphrase it, stating the main theme or story, and then rewrite the poem in their own words. This is fun to do using a traditional poem and changing it into a modern form.

4. Play several musical selections and let students write along with each for a few minutes. For non-writers, play music, then ask them questions, the answers to which could be a poem. For instance, *What color is the music? How does it make you feel? Does it take you somewhere? It is telling a story?* Let them chose a picture to go along with the music. Another technique is to bring in an instrument. Play a short selection and have students draw an outline of the instrument and then write poems inside of their drawings.

5. Have students visualize their imaginations. Ask questions like: *Where does your imagination live? What does it need? When does it do its best work? What would your imagination say if it could talk? What would you want your imagination to do? solve? invent?* Have students write poems that are letters to their imaginations, beginning with the salutation, "Dear Imagination."

Lesson 1   **Using the Five Senses**

Grade: 1-3

Poetic Techniques: Use of the senses to create images, use of similes

Objective
Students will write a five-line poem using all five senses.

Materials
Several objects* that can be easily described in terms of their sensory attributes (color, smell, feel, sound, or visual appearance) placed in a "magic" bag, paper, pencil.

* Objects might be stuffed toy, harmonica, bright ball, fruit, flower, scratch and sniff sticker, piece of bark, or a marble.

Procedure
1. Discuss with students the fact that most people think that poems always have to rhyme, but, in fact, not all poems rhyme. In this lesson they will learn about other elements of poetry. They will write a non-rhyming poem that uses their five senses to describe things.

2. Read one of the suggested poems and ask students to listen for what they can see, hear, feel, taste, or touch in the poem. Use one of the suggested poems at the close of the lesson or choose any poem that has a variety of images for one or more of the five senses.

3. Define **images** as mental pictures of things that are created by describing things using vivid language. Discuss the fact that poets use imagery to make their poems more interesting. Point out the images in the poem(s) that was read and the senses these images appealed to.

4. Pull things out of the bag one at a time and ask students to describe them. Have students be as specific as possible and form comparative statements. For example, they might describe the smell of something not just as *sweet* but as *sweet as a rose;* not just *sour* but *sour like a pickle;* not just *rough* but *rough like sandpaper.* For each item, ask for an adjective to describe one of the object's characteristics. Then ask for a comparison with some other object.

5. Have students write a class poem, describing the class in terms of the five senses. Write the beginning of each line on the board and have students provide the endings.

    Our class tastes like _____
    Our class looks like _____
    Our class feels like _____
    Our class smells like _____
    Our class sounds like _____

6. Have students write their own poems, using the same beginning as the class poem but this time describing their own names. Give students the beginning of each line and have them complete the lines, trying to use language that will create vivid pictures for their readers.

    My name tastes like _____
    My name looks like _____
    My name feels like _____
    My name smells like _____
    My name sounds like _____

7. Read poems. Discuss the images that have been created and the senses that are appealed to.

Follow-up
Write another poem using descriptions and comparisons using the *as* _____ form. For example:

    My class smells as _____ as _____
    My brother looks as _____ as _____
    My name is as _____ as _____

Lesson 1 – Using the Five Senses

Sample Poems

My name tastes like a Snickers bar
My name looks like a sunset
My name smells like a pie
My name sounds like a crisp apple
My name feels like a kitten
　　　　Mrs. Woods' second grade class

My name is as short as an ant
My name is as funky as a skate board
My name is as blaah as a bowl of tomato sauce and peanut butter
My name looks as if it was having a heart attack
My name smells as if it were a skunk
　　　　Katie Benti, second grade

Our class tastes like a hamburger just off the grill
Our class looks like paper dolls
Our class sounds like boiling water
Our class feels slimy
Our class smells like paper
　　　　Mrs. Woods' second grade class

Suggested Poems (use for step 2)

Horny Toad
Here comes a horny toad
Horny, horny, horny toad.

With short stumpy legs
A speckled bumpety back
And buggedy-beady eyes
I put him in my lil' sack
'Cuz he's just about my size
　　　　　　Jane Elsdon

Wind Songs
Whish, whoosh, whish, whoosh!
Whishety, whooshety, whee!
Lish, loosh, lish, loosh!
Lishety, looshety, lee!
Kistles and whistles
And swooshety sing
Such magical sounds
Our friend, the wind, sings!
　　　　　　Jane Elsdon

"My Fingers," in *Knock at a Star*.
"every berry appears edible," in *Under the Bridge of Silence*.

Name _____

All About My Name

Use the space above to write your name in a special way. It can be crazy, fancy, pretty, or bold. Then write a poem about your name.

My name tastes like _____

My name looks like _____

My name smells like _____

My name sounds like _____

My name feels like _____

_____

Write one more line about your name or how you feel about it.

Using the Five Senses
Kindergarten version

Grade: Kindergarten

Poetic Techniques: Forming images based on the senses, rhythm

Objective
Students will participate in writing a five-line poem using all five senses and employing the same number of steady beats in each line.

Materials:
cards with drawings of the five senses on them, five bags (each one labeled with a different sense)*, cards with names and pictures of foods on them*, tape recorder, chalk board or flannel board

* Into each bag, put food cards so that each bag contains a one, two, and three-syllable food word. Put a picture of a sense and a label on the outside of each bag.

Procedure
1. Several days prior to teaching this lesson, introduce students to steady beats by having them listen and move to marching music. Read some poems about food found in Shel Silverstein's books or *Poem Stew*.

2. Read the following poem, listening for the steady beat. Read the poem more than once so students can clap (or tap fingers) along with the beat and identify how many beats are in each line.

   > I can see my hands,
   > I can see my feet,
   > I can smell a rose,
   > I can smell my feet.

3. Review what the five senses are. Tell class that their poem will compare their class to different foods. Each line of the poem will deal with one of our senses and each line will have a steady beat. All lines in the poem will have the same number of beats.

4. Use the following procedure for each of the five senses:
   - Draw three food cards from the bag for that sense.
   - As a group, decide which food to use in the poem.
   - Create a line of the poem using the sense and the food selected.
     Our class____(sense) like ____(food).
   - Clap out beats of the line.
     Make sure all lines have the same number of beats.
   - Write the poem on the chalkboard.
   When finished with the five lines, write one additional summarizing line.

5. If there is time, rehearse the poem several times and then record the class reciting it. Play it back for them to listen to. Prompt recitation with pictures of senses and foods.

6. Review what two things (steady beat and five senses) were used to make the special class poem.

Sample Poem
   Our class looks like beans
   Our class feels like ice
   Our class smells like jam
   Our class tastes like eggs
   Our class sounds like mush
   Yum! Yum! Yum! Yum! Yum!
   Mrs. Freeman's kindergarten class

Name _____

Our Class Is Like

Our class looks like _____

Our class feels like _____

Our class smells like _____

Our class tastes like _____

Our class sounds like _____

_____

Lesson 3   **Doodle Poems**

Grade: K–1

Poetic Techniques: Poems can take any form, use of imagination

Objective: Students will use free association to produce ideas that relate to a non-objective figure and combine these ideas into a doodle poem.

Materials:
crayons, paper and pencil (if you do a group poem or a model poem, use a large piece of poster-sized paper and a marking pen)

Procedure:
1. Draw any kind of simple doodle figure on the board. Brainstorm all the things the drawing could be. Elicit as many answers as possible.

2. Tell students that they can play with words on a page just the way we play with lines and figures (as in doodling). They will be making a big doodle drawing and writing a poem about all the things they see in their drawing.

3. Have students practice drawing doodles on their desks with their fingers. Let one student or a group draw a large doodle on the board or on poster paper. Have students share all the ideas that come to mind then they look at the doodle. Write all suggestions on the large drawing in such a way that they follow the contours of the drawing.

4. Give students paper and tell them to draw a large doodle to fill the page. They can practice drawing with their fingers before they use pencils or crayons. Then have them write all the associations they can think of on the doodle.

    Or

    In cooperative learning groups, have one student draw the doodle, have another student write all the words as they are suggested by other members of the group, another person turn the drawing to show other group members different perspectives, and another student share the poem with the class.

5. Have students share their doodle poems.

Follow-up: Collage poems

Sample Poems

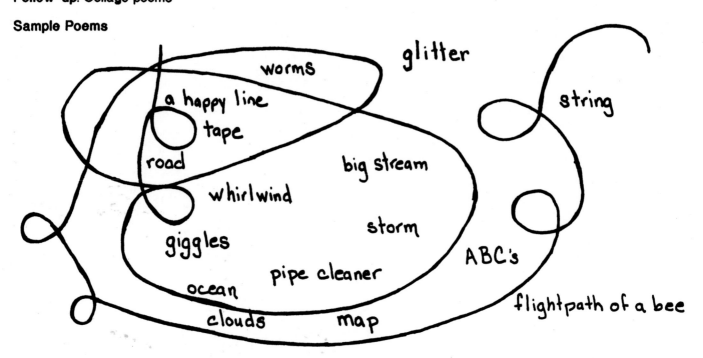

Name _____

My Doodle Poem

Use this space to make one large doodle. When you are finished drawing, write all the words you think of when you look at the doodle. Write as many different words as possible.

Lesson 4

Spring Collage Poem

Image

Grade: K–3

Poetic Techniques: Use of senses to create images, free verse form

Objective
Students will use their five senses to contribute to a group collage poem.

Materials
pictures of collages (from books on artists like Matisse) or actual collages, colored paper cut in shapes to reflect the theme (patterns for a spring theme), wide-tip colored pens, large piece of poster paper, soft music (optional)

Procedure
Note: Depending on the theme you choose for your collage, you will need to alter the elements of the lesson. For example, if your theme is about space, you will want to find poems about space, make cut-out shapes of things related to space, and produce or find a collage with space images.

1.   Show collage. Have students identify what they see in the collage. Ask if they can smell, feel, hear, or taste the collage. Discuss all the things they see in the picture and what story they think the artist was trying to tell.

2.   Tell students that they will be creating a collage and writing a poem to go with it. Before they do this, they will listen to several poems. Read several good poems that are related to your theme. A suggested list of spring poems is at the end of this lesson.

3.   Have students, one at a time, reach into a bag in which you have placed the colored paper shapes of the collage. Then let each student point to the spot on the large piece of paper where he/she wants to place the shape. Glue shape to that spot.

4.   When all shapes are in place, ask students to look at their completed collage. Discuss what they could see, hear, taste, feel, or smell in the collage. Elicit specific rather than general responses. Using a different color of marker pen for each sense, write the words students suggest on the collage. For instance, you might write *birds singing* and all other references to sounds in green, *blue sky* and all references to sights in red, *raindrops* and all other references to things you can feel in orange.

5.   Using the same colored pens as were used to write words that were related to each sense, write "We hear, We see" etc. next to some of the words that students have suggested for the collage. Finally, ask students for one short statement of feeling, like "Spring makes us feel like sunshine." Write the best statement on the bottom of the collage poem.

6.   Read the poem to the class, then read the poem with the class.

Follow-up
Use collage worksheet to have each student complete a drawn collage and write an individual poem.

Sample Poem

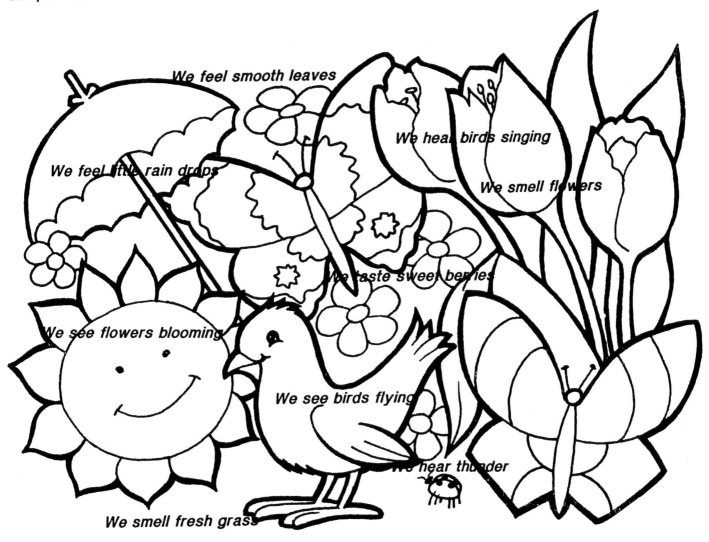

We feel smooth leaves

We hear birds singing

We feel little rain drops

We smell flowers

We taste sweet berries

We see flowers blooming

We see birds flying

We hear thunder

We smell fresh grass

Suggested Spring Poems (use with step 2)

Spring time is here
also the flowers
They also bloom into roses
and daisies
so we could smell
their beautiful scent.
      Andy de la Cruz, fifth grade student

Ride the sunset
into the pink and black sky
Sail over the wide seas
to a land of paradise
Go into the night sky.
      Mary Esser, fifth grade student

"Spring" and "Forsythia Bush" in *Time to Shout*.

"Spring" and "We Like March" in *Talking to the Sun*.

"For Marc Chagall" in *Two Hearts the Color of Flesh*.

Name _____

My Spring Collage Poem

Here is a picture that shows many of the things you would find in springtime. Look at the drawing and then write your thoughts about what you could see, hear, feel, or smell during spring.

I see _____

I hear _____

I smell _____

I feel _____

_____

One sentence that tells how you feel about spring.

Name _____

My Collage Poem

Use this space to make a collage about something. You can draw or paste pictures.

Write a poem about everything you think of when you look at your collage.

_____

_____

_____

_____

_____

Lesson 5   # Simile Poem

Grade: K–3

Poetic Techniques: Use of senses, use of simile, narrative line

Objective
Students will use their five senses to interpret a painting and then contribute to a group poem that is based on the painting and makes use of similes.

Materials
painting, print, or reproduction glued to the center top of a large piece of poster board, tape recorder, and music that is appropriate to the selected picture.

Procedure
1. Show students the picture and ask them to discuss what things they see in the picture. Stress what things all of their senses tell them about the picture. Encourage a variety of interpretations.

2. Give students several examples of similes (comparisons between two things using the words "like" or "as") using examples from the picture. For example, in a circus picture, the white horse might look **like** a cloud or the noise of the drum might sound **like** thunder. Stress the use of the word "like."

3. Make two lists on the chalkboard. In one list write all the things students' senses perceive in the picture. In the other list, write the comparisons. Examples might be:

   We see a dog on a horse   *like a jockey*
   We smell cotton candy   *like perfume*

4. Have students read through the lists of perceptions and comparisons they have created.

5. Ask students to provide lines for a poem that tells about the picture and uses comparisons. As lines are suggested, have other members of the group (either the whole class or small groups) offer comments or suggestions for modification. Once the group agrees on a line, write it on the poster board, directly beneath the picture. If they are working in small groups, have them write their poems on pieces of paper. While they are writing the poem, softly play music that is representative of the mood of the picture.

6. Read the poem to the students. Then have students read the poem with you. If possible, record students reciting the poem and play it back to them.

7. Have students individually select art prints and write their own poems about the picture. Use the worksheet to organize images and write the poem.

Sample Poem
This poem was written about a painting of children at the seaside by the artist Mary Cassat.

The cool, cool ocean sea is like a waterfall
While people swim in the ocean like dolphins.
Sea otters are like hunters of fish.
The sand in my bucket is like gold.
My sister and I are like magic children.

18

Name _____

Simile Poem

Things my senses tell me about the picture .

What these things are like .

_____ like _____

_____ like _____

_____ like _____

_____ like _____

_____ like _____

Here is my poem about the picture

_____

_____

_____

_____

_____

Lesson 6   # Wish Poem

Grade: K–3

Poetic Techniques: Reflection of the real world, use of imaginary elements

Objective
Students will write one or two lines for a class poem using an "I wish" beginning and including both realistic and imaginary elements.

Materials
paper, pencil

Procedure
1. Ask students to think about and share some of their favorite things that they can actually see, touch, hear, smell, and taste. Discuss the fact that these are real things and are part of the real world.

2. Read the following poem and discuss the fact that poems are about the real world. Tell students that poems are like a flashlight in your bedroom in the middle of the night. They light up a part of your world so you see it in a different way. Poets usually write about ordinary things in such a way that they seem special.

>   I look at the shell with no eyes
>   It is smooth with slight ridges
>   It feels like a frozen, closed-up rose
>   I look at the shell with eyes
>   It is shaped in a spiral way
>   It looks like an ice-age rose
>   no color but white
>   beige
>   a rose with no stem
>   nor leaves
>   I listen to it with my eyes
>   I hear small rolling waves in the distance
>   I smell it
>   It smells like salt
>   It is as beautiful
>   as a real rose
>   Christine Hsieh, fifth grade student

4. Tell students that one other element that can be in poems is wishes. They can take something from the real world and wish that it were something different or that it were in some way special. Ask students to share some of the wishes they have made.

5. Give examples of how they can use their imaginations to combine the real world with wishes like *I wish snails were cookies, I wish weeds were fairies* or *I wish erasers could dance.* Ask students to think of some wishes and share them with the class.

6. Read the sample poem.

7. Have students write a wish poem. The lines of their poems should begin with "I wish," combine an element of the real world with creative endings, and be a minimum number of lines (you can set the number). If working with the class as a whole, give students time to think of the lines, then write them on the board. If students are working in pairs or individually, they should write their poems on paper.

Lesson 6 – **Wish Poem**, continued

8. Read poems or have students read poems. As poems are read, ask other students to indicate, by holding up a finger, if poems have each of the following things:
    - lines any way you want (not in standard sentence or paragraph form)
    - rhythm
    - images
    - things from the real world
    - wishes

    The main elements they will use in these poems are the real world and wishes, but some may contain elements of imagery.

Follow-up

Have students take one of their wishes and write a poem describing what happens when the wish comes true. Remind them to use specific images and to be as imaginative as possible.

Sample Poem

I wish fishes were kisses
I wish erasers could dance
I wish pencils were candy
I wish recess was all day
I wish dogs could talk
I wish my hair could get radio reception
I wish today was the first day of summer!
I wish my hat was a helicopter
I wish this poem would write itself
I wish wishes could be ordered over the telephone.

Name _____

Wish Poem

Write a wish poem. Each line should include some real thing and your wish about this object. Use the space above to draw a picture of one of your wishes.

I wish _____

I wish _____

I wish _____

I wish _____

I wish _____

I wish _____

Draw a picture of one of the wishes.

Lesson 7   **Noise Poem**

Grade: 1–3

Poetic Techniques: Use of sense of hearing to create images, onomatopoeia

Objective
Students will write a poem using noise words (onomatopoeia) and other words that are related to noises.

Materials
paper, pencil, noisemakers

Procedure
1. Tell students that they are going to use one sense (hearing) to write poems. They will be writing noise poems that will contain different kinds of noise words. One of these two kinds of words are words that sound like the noises. These are words like *tinkle, buzz, squeak, bang, hiss, clang, cuckoo, crash, slam,* or *purr*. The other kind of words are words that describe noises like *loud, quiet, strong, deafening,* or *soft*. Other words tell how the noises are make like *whisper, shout, blare, cry,* or *moan*.

2. Read a poem, either the one below or some other poem that makes good use of onomatopoeia. Ask students to listen for words that sound like what they are saying.

    > **Wish-Fish**
    > *Ducky swam in the water*
    > *Swooshity, swooshity, swish*
    > *Dove into the swirling depths*
    > *And got his dearest wish*
    >
    > *Ducky swam into the water*
    > *Swooshity, swooshity, swish*
    > *And when he came up again*
    > *He had a first class fish.*
    >   Jane Elsdon

    Other poems that would be appropriate would be in the "Noises" chapter in *Wishes, Lies and Dreams* or "The Skaters" and "Rain" in *Knock at a Star*.

3. Ask students to supply some words that sound like what they are saying (words like *slosh, swoosh, eeek, sizzle, clank, hush, drip, thump, pop, ring, jingle, jangle, tinkle, clink, clang, purr, rat-a-tat, hiss, whoosh, splash,* or *ding dong)*. Write their words on the board. Say the words together.

4. Make a list of other words that are noise words but are not onomatopoeia words; that is, words that do not sound like the sound they are describing. List verbs like *talk, yell, hammer, pound, sing, shout, cry, bark, snort, whisper* and adjectives like *loud, soft, ear-splitting, peaceful, thundering,* or *deafening*.

5. Read one of the sample poems.

6. As a group write a poem using the words students have suggested and whatever other words they would like to add. For the first line of the poem, have students decide where they could be. The first line will set the location. Help students think of noisy places as locations for their poem; for instance, truck or train yards, playgrounds, restaurant kitchens, or a rodeo. Additional lines of the poem should relate to noises that would be heard in this place. Poems can be any length and any form.

7. Have students write their own poems using the same format as the class poem. The first line should tell where they are. Then they should write additional lines using noise words and any additional words they need. Their goal is to make the reader of their poems actually hear the noises in the location they have selected.

8. Read poems aloud. Ask students to choose a favorite sound.

Lesson 7 – Noise Poem

Sample Poems

We are at the circus
Oompah blasts the tuba in the band
Chatter Chatter giggle the monkeys
Roar shouts the lion.

I am in the country
I hear hissing
     Is it a snake?
     Is it a stream?
I hear chirp–chirp
     Is it a bird?
     Is it a frog?
I hear Buzzzzz
     Is it a bee?
     Is it a fly?
I hear yelling
     Is it kids?
I thought the country was quiet
     but now I hear
          Mrs. Thane's first grade class

Follow-up

Present a noise (like a drawer opening and closing, a pencil tapping, environmental sounds on a tape, or paper being crumpled) and have students brainstorm a list of things that make that noise. Students can then use these ideas in a poem, either just rewriting the list or elaborating and adding other words.

Sample Poem

A pencil tapping
sounds like
    rain falling
    my sister practicing her tap dancing
    a metronome
    a clock ticking
    a parking meter running.

Name _____

Noise Poem

Think of a place. Think about all of the sounds you would hear if you were in this place. Write a poem that tells about all of the noises you would hear.

_____

_____

_____

_____

_____

_____

Lesson 8   **"I Know" Poems**

Grade: 1–3

Poetic Techniques: Use of the senses to create images, reflection of the real world

Objective
Students will write a poem describing a familiar scene and using sensory images based on at least three different senses.

Materials
paper and pencil

Procedure
1. Ask students to think about or tell about something they know very well by describing how it looks, smells, tastes, etc. Tell them that they can paint a picture of this thing with words. They can write a poem about this thing they know very well so that the reader will feel that he/she is experiencing the same thing the writer of the poem is experiencing.

2. Read the following poem. Ask students to identify the elements that tell them that it is a poem. Answers might include rhyme, rhythm, images (use of words to create pictures).

> **Pony Song**
> The gray pony sings as he trots to the store
> *Sugar cube, sugar cube, sugar cube, YUM!*
> The white pony hums as he trots to the barn,
> *Oats and hay, oats and hay, HERE I COME!*
>
> The red pony neighs as he runs in the rain
> *Falling drops, falling drops, drops falling free*
> The black pony snorts as he bucks in the rain
> *Falling rain, falling rain, can't catch me!*
> Lani Steele

3. Have students identify the images in the poem by pointing out what senses are appealed to in the poem. For example:
    sight – ponies running and bucking
    touch – the feel of rain
    taste – sugar cube, oats and hay
    hearing – ponies sing, neigh, hum, trot in rhythm
    smell – rain, oats and hay

4. Read one of the sample poems. None of these poems uses rhythm (a steady beat), but students should be able to discuss images that are created and what senses are appealed to.

5. As a group, select a topic that all students are familiar with and write an "I Know" poem that uses all five senses. Use the following format:
    line 1 – "I know (subject)"
    line 2 – Short phrases or sentence about the subject using one of the senses
    line 3 – "I know (subject)"
    line 4 – Short phrases or sentence about the subject using a different sense
    lines 5 – 10 – Same format, using all five senses
    line 11 – An "I know" statement, slightly different from the preceding ones.

6. Discuss some of the topics that students could write a poem about (family, pets, neighborhood, school, a trip, a friend). Then have students write their own "I know" poems. Students should follow the same format as the class poem and should include at least three different senses.

26

Follow-up
Have students write an "I Know" poem about an imaginary place, person, thing, or situation. They could consider writing about a unicorn farm, a black hole, the other side of the rainbow, a secret garden, or a haunted castle. They should still use vivid images.

Sample Poems

I know a long trip in our camper
  My Mom puts her feet up
  Her nose in a book
My Dad says I can't drive and read the map too!
My brother throws little strips of paper out of the window
  He wants Burger King
  I want MacDonald's
I know a long trip in our camper
  If i ask, "Are we there yet?"
  My Mom and Dad both yell,
  "We just started!"
After a while, I fall asleep
  and dream I am swimming
I know a long trip in our camper

I know my dentist's office
  kind waiting people sitting
  in the lobby,
  little bits of blood
I know my dentist's office
  different chemicals
  toothpaste
  cigarette smoke
  teeth being ripped out
  stuffy
    Tara Buck, third grade student

I know my little brother
He looks like the Karate Kid
  Jumps, chops, does the square horse.
I know my little brother
  He has bows and arrows,
  water guns, makes ugly faces
I know my little brother
  At night, he smells like soap
If we see a scary movie
  He sleeps in my bed.
I know my little brother.

Name _____

"I Know" Poem

Write a poem about something you know very well. Choose at least three different senses to describe this thing.

I know _____

_____
    describe your subject using one of the senses

I know _____

_____
    describe your subject using one of the senses

I know _____

_____
    describe your subject using one of the senses

I know _____
    statement different from other "I Know" statements

Lesson 9   # My Neighborhood

Grade: 2-3

Poetic Techniques: Reflection of the real world, use of the senses (especially hearing and sight) to create images

Objective
Students will write a five-line poem on their neighborhood, describing sights and sounds.

Materials
chalkboard, pencil, paper

Procedure

1. Ask students to listen carefully to the sounds in the classroom and to tell you what they hear. Then have them make glasses with their fingers, scan the scene, and tell you what they see. Discuss how we can use poetry to focus on things that we see and hear everyday and usually take for granted. By carefully using our senses, we can notice things that we would normally overlook. These things can be a basis for a poem.

2. Discuss the ways poets often use noises in a poem:
    a) To compare the sound to something else; to tell what the sound is like.
        Practice rattling keys, tapping chalk on a chalkboard, or making noise in some other way. Ask students to make comparisons. They may say things like *keys sound like bells or a window breaking; chalk tapping sounds like a tap dancer or someone knocking on a door.*
    b) To use the sound itself.
        Make a list of some words that sound like the noises they describe (onomatopoeia) that could be used in a poem. This list may include words like *tinkle, crash, splash, pow, baa-baa.*

3. Read one of the sample poems.

4. Ask students to close their eyes and take an imaginary walk through the schoolyard. Then ask them to share some of the things they saw and heard. Try to elicit noise words and noise comparisons when they talk about what they heard. Write ideas on the board as they are shared.

5. As a group write a sample poem on the chalkboard or on a large piece of poster paper using the following format. Stress selecting the observations and sounds that will create a vivid picture for the person who reads the poem.

    > I took a walk today through (the school yard or some other place being observed)
    > I saw. . .
    > I heard. . .
    >   (repeat three for four times)
    > I was surprised (because. . . ., that.. . .)

6. Have students close their eyes and take an imaginary walk through their neighborhoods, paying close attention to sights and sounds. You may wish to have them take notes on what they saw and heard before they start writing their poems. You may also wish to have them write the poem the next day after they have an opportunity to actually walk through the neighborhood.

7. Write individual poems.

8. Read poems aloud.

Follow-up
This type of exercise could be used for a cross-curricular writing assignment. Students could take an imaginary walk through another country (social studies) or an environment (science).
Another variation is to focus on onomatopoeia by having students write a poem using only words that sound like the noise they are describing.

Sample Poem

I took a walk today
   around the same old school
I saw two masks talking to a class
I heard a pencil sharpening
I saw a tetherball through the window
I heard the chain clinking against the pole
I wanted to go outside and play
My eyes, my ears and I were surprised
   that we were so busy
      Mrs. Brown's second/third grade class

Suggested Poems (use with step 3)
"Noise" poems in *Wishes, Lies and Dreams*
"The Beach" and "Boys Walk" in *Teaching Poetry to Children*

Name _____

My Neighborhood

Use these lines to write about all the things you can see and hear in your neighborhood.

I took a walk today through my neighborhood,

I saw _____

I heard _____

I saw _____

I heard _____

I saw _____

I heard _____

I was surprised _____

_____

Lesson 10   **Mask Talk**

Grade: 2, 3

Poetic Techniques: Use of similes

Objective
Students will write poems using similes based on masks presented to them.

Materials
a variety of masks (should be somewhat fantastic rather than realistic), soft music (optional), pencil, paper

Procedure
1. Before showing masks, tell students to remember the first thing they think of when they see the masks. Show the masks one at a time.

2. Select one mask and write some of students' initial reactions on the board. Stress the use of comparisons like "*it looks like____*" or "*it looks as ____ as____.*"

3. Discuss some of the comparisons they have made. Tell them that comparisons are one of the main tools of poetry. Point out that they can use the words *like* and *as* to make these comparisons. You do not have to use the nomenclature of simile except with those children who love big words.

4. Read one of the sample poems.

5. Write a group poem by combining selected lines from step two with any additional words that are necessary to make a poem that describes the mask by making comparisons. Read the lines aloud as a poem.

6. Have students choose one of the masks and write individual poems about the masks or to the masks using as many comparisons as they can.

7. Read the poems, asking other students to listen for comparisons.

Follow-up
Have students write poems speaking as one of the masks. This is using the "voice" in poetry (where the person who is speaking in the poem is not necessarily the voice of the poet). In this way, students can be anyone or anything.

Sample Poems

Cat, you are black like the night
You're supposed to be bad luck
But your whiskers tickle like feathers
Your fur is as soft as velvet
Your purr is like a Maserati motor
You're just a giggle
wrapped up in a black fur!

Coyote, you're so far from the wild
   with your ears like tepees
   and your pointy witch nose
Your eyes like the car headlights
   that reflect in them
Jump! Coyote!
People are shooting your bothers
   like fish in a barrel

Suggested Poems (use before presenting lesson)
"you can look into my face" in *Crazy to Be Alive in Such a Strange World*.
"Racoon" in *Knock at a Star*.

Name _____

Mask Talk

Write a poem about a mask. Describe the mask by comparing it to other things. Draw a picture of your mask.

_____

_____

_____

_____

_____

_____

Comparison Poems Using Names

Poetic Techniques: Use of similes, acrostic form, use of adjectives

Objective

Students will complete an acrostic poem using their names to form the first letter of each line. Each line will be a simile.

Materials

pencil, paper

Procedure

1. An acrostic is a poem in which the first letter of the lines of the verse spell a name or message. Write an acrostic poem (either the one below or one of your choice) on the chalkboard. Ask students what they notice about it. Who is named in the poem? (answers: Mighty Mouse and Amber)

   Mighty, like a giant
   Over us all, like the sky
   Useful, like a sword of right
   Slippery, like a fly
   Excellent, like a shining light
   Oh, brilliant rodent light!

   A smile like a cheshire cat
   My feet are sneaky like sneakers
   Books are special, like friends
   Excellent, like Flo Jo, at running
   Ripe, like an apple

2. Read one of the poems above or the following poem, noting comparisons that have been made.

   Limber, like a puppy chasing its tail
   Active, like a washing machine
   Naughty, like a grin
   Independent, like the Fourth of July
      Lani follows her own path

3. Ask students for the name of someone they would like to write about. Write the name vertically on the chalkboard. Create a group poem by having students suggest lines to correspond to each letter in the name, making comparisons using the word *like*. The last line of the poem can be a summation without the *like* comparison.
   Note:
   For very young students, any apt comparison is satisfactory. With older or more skilled students, try to have them create lines that work together to create a portrait.

4. Have students write their own names vertically down the edge of a piece of paper. They will use the letters in their name to create a poem about themselves using the *like* comparison in each line, choosing characteristics that describe them or that they wish they had. Remind them to add one last line to complete their poem. This line does not have to use a comparison.

Follow-up

1. Use the *as* or *as _____ as* (pink as a sea shell, as big as a house) instead of the *like* comparison.
2. Instead of an acrostic, let students begin each line with *My name is like* or *my name is as___ as*

3. Third grade students may be ready to try metaphors, making comparisons without the words *like* or *as*. Have students think about their special qualities by choosing three things that best stand for or represent them. They may write individual poems or a group poem, like the one below.

   Sample Poem
   Laura is a spider climbing a web, looking for heaven
   Carol is a song singing to herself
   Jeremy is an arrow to the stars
   Matthew is a sturdy bear in a deep wood
   Kevin is a Maserati going 100 miles an hour

Name _____

Name Poem

Moves like a panther,
Inquisitive as a cat,
Clever as a spy,
M
I
C
H
A
E
L

Write your name down the side of this piece of paper so that one letter is on each line. Using these letters as the beginning, write lines of a poem to describe yourself. Make a comparison in each line using the words *like* or *as*.

_____

_____

_____

_____

_____

_____

_____

_____

Songs Our Names Sing

Poetic Techniques: Language poetry (deconstruction), using sounds, jazz poetry, free association

Objective
Students will write poems using rhythm, sounds, and images derived from the syllables of their names.

Materials
paper, pencil

Procedure
1. Read the following poem to students, asking them to listen to and be able to tell you the poet's name. (answer: Shauna)

   > SH sh sh shush up
   > SH sh sh oh my
   > Au au au oh my
   > Au au au oh no
   > Na na na like a goat
   > Na na na what will I do
   > Na na na na do not know
   > Na na not know what to do

2. Discuss how this poet used her name to write a poem. Specifically, she took it apart and used the sounds. The name was divided to get the sounds that were desired, not necessarily into correct syllables.

3. Ask students to write their names on paper, look at them, and play with the sounds in their names. Model different ways of extracting sounds from a name on the board. For example:

   > **Barbara** could be:
   > *Ba/r–r–/bar–r–/ahhhh* or
   > *Bar/bar/ah* or
   > *B/are/b/are/ah*

   The critical part of this lesson is that students feel comfortable dividing their names into units of sound. These units do not have to correspond to the syllables of their names. Show students how to divide names using slashes and have them try two or three different ways to divide their names. Be sure that students have done this step before they write their poems.

4. Once students have had a few minutes to look at their names, ask them to think about how they could make a poem out of these sounds. Model with one or two students' names or read some of the sample poems. The idea behind these poems is something like scat singing. Students may try to make sense out of the sounds or just play with the sounds.

5. Have students write their own poems based on the sounds in their names. If some students really enjoy this exercise, they may write a poem for both their first and last names.

6. Have students read their poems.

Follow-up
Lesson 13, **Rhythm of Our Names**, is an excellent follow-up for this lesson. Students use their names again as a basis for writing poems using two types of rhythm. The use of the sounds in their names in this lesson will, consciously or unconsciously, augment their work in lesson 13.

Sample Poems

Tyson
Pre-writing exercise
T/y/sss/on
Ty/son
Ty/sss/on

Sample poems
Ty tie tie like a knot
  in a rope
Ty tight
Sss, don't slip
On, on a banananana!

T, like T-ball
Y, why do I do it?
Sssss, a slippery slider got by
On, who's on first?

Jessica
Pre-writing exercise
J/ess/ic/ca

Sample Poem
J in my name comes jumping
Gee!
Ess slips in like a small wind
Ick - what's an ick? Sticky ice cream, and
Ca, like call, call me on the phone
Call me to dinner
  at home

Name _____

Songs Our Names Sing

Use this space to write your name and then to divide it into sounds.
Try several different ways to divide your name.

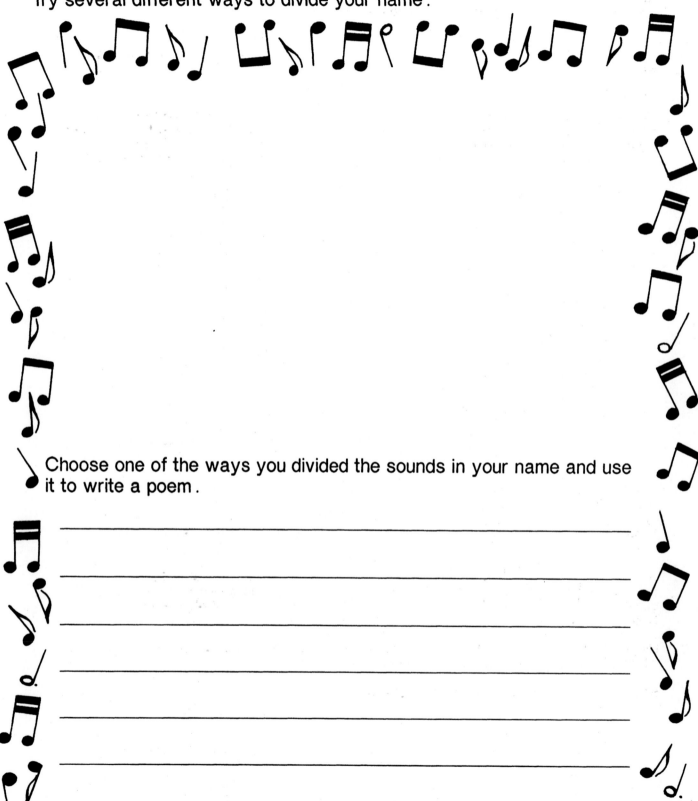

Choose one of the ways you divided the sounds in your name and use it to write a poem.

_____

_____

_____

_____

_____

_____

_____

Lesson 13

The Rhythm of Our Names

Grade: 3

Poetic Techniques: rhythm (steady beat and cadence)

Objective
Students will write a poem using the rhythmic pattern of their names.

Materials
paper, pencil, small drum or other percussion instrument (optional), long scarf or piece of material (optional)

Procedure

1. Discuss the fact that some poems have a rhythm that is a steady beat; a beat you can walk or march to. Read the following poem. Ask students to listen carefully the first time it is read. Read it a second time. This time have students tap their fingers quietly on their desks in time to the steady beat. Have them repeat the bunny's name, noticing that it has a beat they could march to.

   > Hip Hop is my bunny
   > He's white as falling snow
   > He's sweet as clover honey
   > When he sniffs-snoffs with his nose!

2. Tell students that some rhythm patterns are more like a tree swaying in the wind or water bubbling over stones in a brook. You don't march to these rhythms, but you might sway to them. Usually the accents are not regular and repeating. Read the following poem. Encourage students to feel the motion of the poem. Read the poem a second time and let students sway to the rhythm or give them a scarf and let them wave it in time to the lines.

   > My bunny's as white as snow, or stars
   > Her nose goes all day, like a flashing pink sign
   > She signals me with her ears:
   >   Up like flags means she is happy
   >   Down like empty shirt sleeves shows me she is sad
   >   Ears in her dish means
   >   dirty ears!

3. Ask students to think about their names. Is theirs a swaying name, a marching name or a little of both? Help students with examples of a few of their names, determining which are swaying and which are marching names. For example, Bobby Forsythe is a marcher, Felicia Montgomery sways. Kevin Hartigan marches, but Billy Meriweather slows and begins to sway in mid-stride. Give students time to play with their names.

4. Read sample poems. Have students tap out the beats in the poem that uses a steady beat (Kevin Stone).

5. As a group write two sample poems — one for a name that has a steady beat and one for a name that has a swaying rhythm. Once names have been selected, have students offer lines that will carry out the same beat as the name. The poems may be in any form. Write the poems on the board.

6. Have students write their own poems. Before beginning, check to make sure each person knows whether his or her name has a steady beat or a swaying rhythm.

7. Read poems aloud or have students read poems.

Follow-up

If the class has been successful with Lessons 12 and 13, you could combine the concepts to write a name poem using both the rhythmic and sound elements of the name to make a scat song. These poems do not need to make sense as they are just playing with rhythm and the sounds of language. Here is an example:

> LA in my name is like a song
> la la la la
> NI is like bees seeing knees on trees
> no fees please
> CA is caring sharing a soaring caw
> crow caw far and near
> ROL is tootsie roll or cinnamon
> roll is the early morning train

Sample Poems

Alicia Margaret Montgomery
 is embroidery on a pillow edged in lace
Alicia Margaret Montgomery dances a slow dance
  everywhere she goes
  No one calls her Allie, Maggie, or Mont
 not ever
Alicia Margaret Montgomery is like a pink stone
  shining among dark rocks
  under a shining
  rushing
  river

Kevin Stone
knows his mind
throw the ball
like a flash
Kevin Stone
quick to see
loves his dog
likes to fish
Kevin Stone
hates to write
That is me
Kevin Stone

Name _____

The Rhythm of Our Names

Does your name have a steady beat or a swaying pattern? Say it to yourself several times. Is it more like clapping or more like swaying?

Use this space to write a poem that uses your name and the same rhythm pattern of your name.

_____

_____

_____

_____

_____

_____

Lesson 14

Animal Dreams

Grade: 2, 3

Poetic Techniques: Use of senses, poetic voice (who is talking in the poem)

Objective
Students will write a poem describing the dream of a wild or domestic animal in either the first or third person, using images based on the five senses.

Materials
paper, pencil, pictures of domestic and wild animals

Procedure
1. Put up pictures of as many different kinds of animals as possible around the room.

2. Ask students how many of them have seen a dog or cat sleeping. Discuss what animals do when they are sleeping (twitch, make noises, move their feet). What might animals be dreaming about?

3. Ask students to close their eyes while you read one of the following poems. Ask them to try to see the poems in their imaginations. Who or what is the poem about? Where is it happening? What images can they see or feel with their senses?

> Dog of mine has eyes
>   that shine like silver stones
> in the dark and loves to eat bones
> She dreams of beautiful water
>   that sparkles like gold
> She dreams of herself
>   eating hundreds of bones
> She dreams that she was
>   in a beautiful forest, under a tree
> She dreams that her owner
>   could know what the dog
>   was saying
>   Sara Schuh, third grade

> A pony dreams
>   of winning a race
> wearing flowers so sweet
>   tasting oats and sugar cubes
> This pony's feet move in his sleep
>   He feels the silky blue ribbon
> against his cheek, hears the roar
>   of the crowd, the soft murmur
> of the girl who rides
>   A pony dreams
>   of winning a race
> this pony's feet
>   move fast in his sleep
>   Lani Steele

Another poem that could be used is "The Sloth" in *Collected Poems of Theodore Roethke*.

4. Write a poem as a group. Poems can be in any form and any length. First determine the following things:
   - what animal to use
   - where the animal will be in the dream
   - whether you will be telling the dream as the animal or telling about the animal's dream
   - what the animal can see, hear, feel, smell, or taste in the dream
   - how the animal makes you feel (what emotion does it elicit?)

5. Tell students to select one animal and write a poem about that animal's dream. Remind them to include all of the things that were included in the group poem.

6. Read poems aloud or have students read their own poems.

Follow-up
Most students really enjoy this poetry exercise, so you can repeat it by having students select another animal to write about.

Name _____

Animal Dreams

Choose an animal that you would like to write a poem about. Write a poem about a dream this animal is having. Think about where the dream is happening and what the animal can see, feel, hear, taste, and touch in the dream.

_____

_____

_____

_____

_____

Animal Comparison Poems

Poetic Technique: Use of similes

Objective
Students will write poems comparing an animal to other things, using the word "like."

Materials
pencil, paper, common classroom objects

Procedure

1. Hold up a common classroom object. Ask students to tell you about the object by describing its attributes or characteristics. Write these on the board under the heading of "properties." Then ask them to compare this thing to other things by telling you what these attributes are like. Put the comparisons in a separate list on the board

    Example for a piece of paper

Properties	Comparison
white – color	like snow, ice, a cloud
rectangle – shape	like a door, a window, a coffin
flat – dimension	like film, the chalkboard
rattles – noise	like twigs in the wind, like baby's rattle
write on it – use	like the chalkboard

    Do a couple of these comparisons with common objects.

2. Tell students that they'll be working on comparisons in their poetry. Review the properties or characteristics of things that can be used for comparisons (size, shape, color, smell, taste, uses, behavior, etc.)

3. Ask students to try to compare some unusual things:
    - How is a mouse like an elephant?
    - How is something inside the classroom like something outside?
    - How is a glass like a shoe?
    - How is the wind like a telephone?

4. Read a poem that contains comparisons or one of the sample poems. Some good poems for this lesson are "The Magnificent Bull", "The War God's Horse Song", and "Autumn Cove", all in *Talking to the Sun*. You should, however, be able to find many good examples of the use of similes in any poetry anthology.

5. Write a group poem comparing an animal to several different things. Let the group choose the animal for the class poem. The poem should give the name of the animal and state several characteristics of the animal. Each characteristic should be compared to some other thing using the word "like"

6. Have students write their own poems independently. Remind them to make as many unusual comparisons as they can and to really think about all the characteristics and behaviors of their animal before they begin, so they will have many ideas for several comparisons.

8. Read poems aloud.

Follow-up
Students can do comparisons of animals using the "as ___" or the "as ___ as" form. For example:

> a bear is as fierce as a warrior
> a bear, brown as his mud hole

Following that, you may want to try comparisons without the words "as" (metaphors). This is usually a difficult concept for primary children, but some can do it, and love it. For example:

> the bear, fierce warrior of the forest
> the bear, a walking brown mud hole

Sample Poems

an elephant
   wrinkled like a messy bed
   gray like clouds
   big like a tree
   makes loud noises like a trumpet
he is fat like a hula hoop
he is from the African jungle
   like lions
What does he do all day?

The frog is green
   like a tree
The frog hops
   like a cricket
The frog has big eyes
   like my sister
The frog is small
   like a mouse
The frog can swim
   like a fish
It's baby is like a fish, but
   it grows up four-legged
   like a horse
It croaks
   like a foghorn
It eats flies, like toads
   then it croaks

Name _____

My Animal Poem

Choose an animal. Think about what the animal is like. Write a poem that describes the animal by comparing its characteristics to other things by using the word *like*.

_____

_____

_____

_____

_____

_____

Lesson 16   # Alphabet Poems

Grade: 2, 3

Poetic Techniques: Language poem, playing with the elements of language, new perspectives of familiar things

Objective
Students will write a poem about a letter of the alphabet by using all five senses and looking at the letter in new ways.

Materials
pencil, paper, chalkboard

Procedure
1. Draw a letter M on the board. Ask students for some suggestions of what the letter could be. Elicit creative answers like *two mountains, trees, two party hats, a valley, half of a zig zag*. Then draw an upside-down M. Elicit associations like *ice cream cones, fold-up bed*. Draw a sideways M. Ask students what it looks like. Encourage creative responses again, like *the letter E, two noses, directional arrows,* or *sideways mountains*. Tell students that there are lots of ways of looking at things besides the one we're used to. Today they will be looking at and thinking about letters in different ways.

2. Read suggested poems. Ask students to picture what is happening and to draw a picture on their desks with their fingers of the letters in the second and third poems.

3. Choose a letter for the group poem. Draw the letter on the chalkboard in each position. Elicit several answers from students for each of the following questions. Write responses on the chalkboard.
   - What does it look like standing in its regular position?
   - What does it look like on its side?
   - On the other side (if different)?
   - How does it look upside down?
   - Do you have an idea how this letter might smell or taste?
   - How would it feel (sharp, soft, etc.)?
   - What does this letter sound like (NOT words starting with the letter)?
     For example:

     > T says tuh tuh tuh
     > What does that remind you of?
     > rain drops hitting earth, pencil tapping

     > R says Rrrrrrrrrr
     > lion, motorboat

   - What are some good things that start with this letter?
   - What are some scary things that start with this letter?

4. Using student input, write a poem that includes ideas or responses from step 3. Arrange lines in the most interesting order, delete repetitions, add lines where necessary. Read aloud.

5. Have students follow these guidelines to write their individual letter poems:
   - Each student chooses a letter.
   - On the back of their papers, draw their letter as a capital as big as the page.
   - Look at the letter for a least two minutes. Turn the page on its side and upside down.
   - Listen to its sound. What does that sound remind you of? What words begin with this letter?
   - Write the poem.
   - Draw a picture of the letter.

Sample Poems

E looks like a two-story garage
E sounds like a scream in a bat cave
EEEEEEEEEEEEEEEEEE
E tastes like eggplant, yuck
E smells like exhaust
E feels like a hand poking
E upside down looks like a three-legged racer
E sounds like echoes

A sounds like AAAH, for the doctor
A looks like a mountain, or a rocket
A on its side looks like an arrow: this way!
A upside down is a falling bomb
A feels like a roller coaster, UP then DOWN
I like A because it's always first

Suggested Poems (Use with step 2)

Poem 1

I got in line for ice cream
I'm first! he cried
I'm here! he yelled
I want it right now! he bellowed

But **M** marched through on three mighty
muddy feet
Calling, Me first! Me here! Me want it now!
and stomped poor I into the sidewalk.

P persisted politely
Please give me peach and pistachio
and hopped away licking his cone.

Poem 2

There once was a guy who swallowed a Y
A bright yellow Y
I don't know why

I don't know how
But the guy with a bow
ate that Y upside down
and look at him now!

Well, I am that guy
I am the fellow
who yesterday swallowed that bright yellow letter.
Now I feel better:
I stand on my head
with my feet to the sky
doing yoga in yellow

Poem 3

R rolled over –
but then he got stuck

48

Name _____

Alphabet Poem
Planning Page

- Write your capital letter on the back of this page. Make it as big as possible.
- Turn the page around to see your letter from all angles.
- Answer the following questions about your letter. Be creative.

1. What sound does your letter make (not words that begin with it)?

   _____

2. What does the letter taste like?

   _____

3. What does the letter smell like?

   _____

4. What does the sound remind you of?

   _____

5. What does your letter look like?

   _____

6. What does it feel like?

   _____

7. What are some good words that begin with this letter?

   _____

8. What special things can this letter do?

   _____

Name _____

Alphabet Poem

N O R D L E S A H O J E
U B A
D B A E E S U J L
C N H O J L
N L Y Q
W L R
A
T N S
C R S

Use this space to write your poem about a letter. Use the space above to draw a picture of your letter and one of its adventures.

_____

_____

_____

_____

_____

_____

50

Lesson 17   # Dinosaur Poems

Grade: 2, 3

Poetic Techniques: Voice, use of senses

Objective
Students will write a poem incorporating information about dinosaurs to create a voice as one kind of dinosaur.

Materials
pencil, paper, pictures of dinosaurs and their habitats, models of dinosaurs or toy dinosaurs

Procedure
1. Tell students you are going to read two poems; their job is to use the clues in the poems to guess what kind of dinosaur each poem is about.

What has my lovely neck to do
  with this hugeness of my body?
Too heavy for earth,
  I plant my legs under water
  like drowned trees
They support the island of me
  while my neck
  that snake of the air
    is seeking the heights

answers: A large long-necked, plant-eating
dinosaur like diplodocus or brontosaurus

I am king of teeth
  see them gleam
  hear them click gently
  like insects
Then crash, like
  the terrible exploding mountain
Do not let me catch
  your scent
  in this heavy air
My teeth are hungry

answer: Tyrannosaurus Rex or allosaurus

2. Ask students what they could learn about the dinosaurs' world from the poems. What did they hear? Read the poems again if necessary.

3. Tell students that in poetry, voice refers to who is talking in the poem (not necessarily the voice of the poet). They will pretend that they are dinosaurs and write a poem in the voice of the dinosaur.

4. Write the five senses (sight, hearing, touch, taste, smell) on the chalkboard, leaving room for a column under each sense. Tell students that in order to make their poems real, they need to think about the world dinosaurs lived in. Under each sense, elicit examples from students of things the dinosaur might see, hear, smell, taste, touch.

5. Without writing, have a brief discussion about how it would feel to be a dinosaur. How would stegosaurus feel with all those plates on his back? Does it like to swish its tail around and fell trees? What else might it like to do?

6. As a group, choose a dinosaur for the class poem. Using the words in the list from step 4 and the discussion as a basis, write a five to seven line poem. Start poem with "I (name of dinosaur)" and add other lines to describe the dinosaur's surroundings and feelings.

7. Read the poem together.

8. Write the names of several dinosaurs on the chalkboard. Have students choose a dinosaur (a different kind of dinosaur than in class poem) to write a poem about. It should be at least five lines. All poems should begin "I (name of dinosaur)". They can use words in the lists from step 4 and any additional references and words they can think of.

9. Read student poems.

10. Review with students what **voice** in poetry is (who is talking in poem) and whose voice they wrote in (a dinosaur's).

Follow-up
A pirate poem can be presented in essentially the same manner. Read aloud some of your favorite poems or even prose about pirates. Discuss the usual surroundings of a pirate. What would it feel like to be Long John Silver or Blackbeard? Have students write poems in which they are the pirates.

Sample Poems

I, Triceratops
 sit on my eggs, patiently
 guarding them
Tyrannosaurus Rex,
 who everyone calls
 Sharp Tooth
is scrounging around
 these swamps
He's looking for my eggs
 Oh, no! He's here
I'll fight to save my eggs
 One big push
 to the cliff
I won! He's over the edge!
         Valerie Kaplan, fourth grade student

I, Stegosaurus
 hear the stomp of
Tyrannosaurus Rex
 I feel the ground shaking
from the black-smoke mountain
 I smell the blood of my cousins
and the stink water of the swamp
 I fear the sharp teeth of the
Allosaurus, even though my skin
 is as tough as trees.
         Danielle Silveira, fourth grade student
             and Lani Steele

Name _____

Dinosaur Poem

Pretend that you are a dinosaur. Then write a poem about what it is like to be this dinosaur.

_____

_____

_____

_____

_____

_____

_____

Swing Poems

Lesson 18

Grade: 1–3

for the Korean Dano Holiday, May 5

Poetic Technique: Use of senses, using multi-cultural sources

Objective

Students will write a poem in which he/she imagines him/herself swinging (at the Dano spring festival). The poem will use one or more of the five senses.

Materials

paper, pencil

Procedure

1. Ask students how many love to swing. Ask them to close their eyes and imagine that they are swinging in a swing hung from a large tree. Have them describe how it feels when they are swinging.

2. Tell students that they will be using their imaginations to take a trip to Korea and writing a poem about their trip. Show them Korea on a world map. It is near China and Japan, and its people are Oriental. Their customs are similar, but not the same as, Japanese and Chinese customs. Explain that the Dano holiday in Korea is celebrated on May 5 to celebrate the coming of spring. During this holiday, girls dress up in beautiful old-fashioned dresses called hanboks. All the children play, and the girls swing together on swings hung high from tall trees. In their bright dresses, they look like butterflies (try to elicit this image from children).

3. Read "The Swing" by Robert Louis Stevenson in *A Child's Garden of Verses* or one of the following poems.

    > When I swing I'm part of the sky
    > and the galaxies, swirling around
    > seeing Earth, sky
    > Earth, sky
    > I think I may shoot out into space like a star
    > hear the rush of the air in my ears
    > as I fly on to outermost space
    > Only my stomach left behind on Earth
    > shrunk, sunk, and dizzy.

    > Not in heaven, not on earth
    > But you are in mid-sky
    > Blue hills and green waters
    > Seem to swing to and fro
    > You come as falling flowers
    > You go as skimming swallows
    > > an ancient Korean poet

4. Ask students to think about spring: how it smells, tastes, feels, what it looks like, and what it sounds like. Ask them to close their eyes and imagine that they are swinging high in a tree in springtime. They can be in Korea at the Dano celebration or in some other surroundings. Ask them to pay attention to what their senses tell them about their surroundings.

5. Discuss and write on the board some of the images that students experience when they are swinging.

6. Read a sample poem.

7. Write a model poem with the class. You can use any form, but the poem should have at least five lines, should include at least one sense, and should end with an expression of feeling (how they feel about their swinging or their surroundings).

8. Students can write their own poems, either individually, in pairs, or in cooperative groups.

9. Read poems aloud or have students read their poems.

Lesson 18 - **Swing Poems**, continued

Follow-up
This exercise could be used with any culture you want to examine or write about by asking students to imagine that they are in the environment and then putting the things they would experience into a poem.

Sample Poems

I am going so high up in the air
I see birds going high up in the air
It is so high
It feels so going
It feels so going
      Jaime Maier, first grade student

Deer are all around you
When you are swinging
Up high the air smells good
      Megan Goodman, first grade student

I am swinging up so high
  with the blue sky
Korea swing high in the air
I can swing so high
The birds sing nice
The air smells nice
I swing high up
  in the air
    at Korea
I have fun
      Mr. Coulston's first grade class

Name _____

Swing Poem

Use this space to write a poem about swinging. Include lines that tell what you would see, hear, taste, smell, or feel when you are on a swing.

_____

_____

_____

_____

_____

_____

_____

a line telling how you feel about swinging

Naming a New Constellation

Lesson 19

Grade: 2, 3

Poetic Technique: Use of imagery

Objective
Having made a new constellation, students will name it and write a poem describing the constellation or telling how it developed.

Materials
paper, pencil, black paper, glue-on stars, sample constellation picture

Procedure
1. Before you teach this lesson, set the mood for it by reading "Escape at Bedtime" by Robert Louis Stevenson in *A Child's Garden of Verses* or "Moon" or "Why is the Sky Dark?" in *Thread Winding in the Loom*.

2. Ask students if they know the names of any constellations. Write the names on the board. Discuss why constellations are named for things like the dog or the hunter. Ask students what they see when they look at the stars. Tell them that in this lesson they will have a chance to name their own constellations.

3. Read one of the sample poems.

4. Using your sample constellation picture, study the shape, decide on a name and as a group write a model poem on the chalkboard. Before writing, decide if the poem will describe the constellation or tell how it came to be or both. Either elicit lines from the class as a whole or have groups work together to contribute one line per group. The poem can be any form. When finished, read the group poem together.

5. Give each student a number of stars and have them drop them on a piece of black paper, glue the stars where they fall, and then turn the page to look at the design from different angles. After they decide what their constellation looks like, they can name it.

6. Have students write their own poems about their own constellations. Poems should be five or six lines long but can be any form.

Sample Poems

Laabosn Vex hangs high
  a gold and silver necklace
  around summer's western sky
Two shimmering wavy-curvy lines
  with silver pendants too
She sings of travel around and through
  the tunnels of time
  the caverns of space
Another place
is Laaboson Vex
for me, for you

She lives!
See how she stretches her starry tail to the east
See how her reddish eye watches us
to swat us into another galaxy
As far, as cold and old
  as the cat of an Egyptian goddess
which once she was

Keith
  victim of TV-itis, lies
  on the rug, hypnotized
  wishing to be skymaster
An ad: "Call for your wish"
Keith calls the guy
  wishes for sky
Returning parents find
  an empty rug
From the sky, Keith sees
  family car go by
Police know nothing, until
  the nightly news: Keith in the sky!
Watching, nightly news
  Keith, in the sky
Watches satellite, starvision, Sky TV

        Mrs. Emmons' third grade class

Name _____

Constellation Poem

Write a poem about your constellation. You can describe the constellation or tell about how it came to be and where it is located.

_____

_____

_____

_____

_____

_____

_____

Lesson 20   # Holiday Poems
Grade: K–3

Holidays provide excellent opportunities to write many different kinds of poems. Students are usually excited before a holiday, and a poem gives them a different kind of language experience with which to express their enthusiasm. The following are several different ideas for using holidays as a basis for poetry writing.

Procedure

1. **Holiday Acrostics**
   Write the name of the holiday vertically on the chalkboard or worksheet. Then have students write objects, actions, or feelings associated with the holiday on each line so that the first word in each line begins with the letter for that line. Stress use of the poetic techniques that have been introduced like use of the senses or use of similes to form comparisons.

   Sample Poem

   Thank goodness for turkey   Juicy, like watermelon
   Hot and delicious   Up above, fireworks
   And cool ruby cranberries   Lazy, like summer
   No sweet potatoes, please   Yell: Happy Birthday America!
   Kinsfolk gather around   4   You and me!
   Sing our thanks loudly
   Giving unto others, too
   Ice cream and pumpkin pie
   Very delicious
   In a little while
   Nothing will be left
   Going home happy

2. **Holiday ABC Poem**
   Have students write several consecutive letters of the alphabet. Then have them select and write words, feelings, objects and actions associated with the holiday. For each word that is listed, have students write additional words associated with that word.

   Sample Poem

   Halloween ABC's

   Apple   bite teeth crunch
   Boo!   Aaaaaah!
   Cat   black meowww!
   Doorbell   Trick or Treat
   Eat   candy apples gum
   Frightening   witches goblins
   Ghosts   Ooooooh!
   Halloween   It's fun
   It's scary   I feel good!
        Trick or Treat!
        Mrs. Freeman's kindergarten class

3. **Holiday Colors**
   List colors that come to mind for the holiday. Then write items associated with each color.

   Sample Poem

   Christmas is red
   red as holly berries
   red as cranberry sauce
   red as Santa's nose

   Fourth of July is red, white and blue
   like the flag on a blue pole
   like a barber pole
   like George Washington's hat

4. **Holiday Feelings**
Have students write feelings that are associated with the holiday or similes that compare the holiday to actions and things associated with the holiday.
   Sample Poem
   Valentine's Day feels like love
     it feels like giving and getting something wonderful
     It feels like caring

   Valentine's Day feels like lace
     it feels like chocolate melting in your mouth
     it feels like envelopes in your hand

5. **Shape Poems**
Cut out or draw a shape associated with the holiday (a heart for Valentine's Day, a tree for Christmas, a turkey for Thanksgiving, etc.). Write around the shape with words associated with the holiday.

6. **Holiday Monster Poems**
Have students invent monsters, each part of which is a noun associated with the holiday.
   Sample Poem

Christmas Monster:	Fourth of July Monster:
candy cane legs	cherry bomb nose
cranberry eyes	fountain arms and legs
turkey body	hot dog fingers
presents for arms	beach ball body
gift box feet	snake eyes
pine needle hair	strawberry shortcake face
ornament face	always popping off!

7. **Adaptations**
You can make up specific lessons for any holiday using many of the formats that have been presented in this book. In addition to usual holidays, you can use non-American holidays for cross-cultural or multi-cultural education or you can even make up holidays.

Additional Classroom Activities

Writing Across the Curriculum

1. Science provides some beautiful images (stars, amoebae, plants, the body) on which to base poetry. Have students describe a process (a plant growing, a star imploding), go inside an object and describe it (inside a shell, a rose, a rock, or a twig), or be an object from the science study.

2. Create a poem based on some situation from the social studies curriculum. Ask students to imagine that they are in a particular situation (like a Native American village 500 years ago). Give them pertinent information. Then have them write a poem about the location or from the perspective of someone in this situation.

3. Translation/forced image poems are created by using a vocabulary unfamiliar to students, either from a foreign language or an advanced vocabulary in their own language. The basic procedure is as follows:

   a. Have students write a descriptive poem of a place, an event, or something of local importance.

   b. Have them strike out one or more words in each line of their poems and replace the words with ones selected from the foreign language list.

   c. Provide students with translations or definitions of the foreign words and have them rewrite the poems with the new words in English. The forced images that result are always interesting, often poetic, and sometimes inspired.

   Example:

Original Poem	Replacement with Spanish words
In the dark bay, the gray fog loses itself	In the bailano bay, the rosa fog loses itself

   Translation
   In the dancing bay, the pink fog loses itself

4. Another kind of translation poem is changing from traditional poetry to free verse. It is usually best to include an intermediate step of translating the poetry into a prose synopsis of the story or sense of the poem, then rewrite it into modern form.

   Example
   Little Miss Muffett
   Sat on her tuffet
   Eating her curds and whey.
   Along came a spider,
   And sat down beside her,
   And frightened Miss Muffett away.

   Synopsis
   A little girl sat on a grassy mound eating her cottage cheese a long time ago. A spider came up and scared her away.

   Model Poem
   A long-ago little girl
   Eating creamy cheese while
   Sitting on a pillow of green grass
   Saw hairy black legs and shiny eyes
   And ran like the wind
   From the spider
   Who only wanted someone to eat lunch with her!

Publishing and Recognizing Student work

1. It is extremely advantageous to publish student poetry in even the simplest format. Students are greatly motivated by seeing their work in print.

2. Broadsides are single pages with one or several poems on them. They are easy to produce in the age of computers and quick printing. These publications are encouraging to student writers.

3. A chapbook is a 81/2 by 11 inch paper that is folded in half to make a book that is 51/2 inches wide and 81/2 inches tall. It is usually stapled, but can be sewn or put in spring binders. These books have the advantage of being able to arrange poems to best show them off. Illustrations can be added.

4. Poetry readings can be a fun outlet for students. Start with students reading their poems to one another in class. Then organize a reading for another class. You can group poems around a theme or simply present poems that students have written. Readings are an excellent opportunity to work on both speaking and listening skills.

5. Audio and video taping is a favorite with students. The clue to a shining performance is rehearse, rehearse, rehearse. It is not only fun, but this gives students insight into how their poems sound.

6. Have all students write poetry about one theme. Then combine the poems to make a calendar that has several student poems and illustrations for each month. This way, students will have poems to read throughout the year.

Silly Poems
1. Telephone poems are based both on the Japanese chain-poem (renga) and the children's party game. Write a line at the top of a page. Give the paper to a student. The student writes a line of a poem, folds the paper so that only the line that he/she wrote is showing, and gives the paper to another student. Continue the same procedure until several people have added to the poem. Read the poem when it is completed. These poems are fun. Everyone has a style, and students will learn to recognize others' work even in just one line.

2. Limericks are fun, and once students know the rules for limericks, they can't be stopped. Give a starting line and a limited amount of time for writing and have each student write a poem using this beginning line. Students could work individually or in groups. Limericks can be based on local events or persons. The rules for limericks are that in the five-line poem, lines one, two and five rhyme, and the shorter lines (three and four) rhyme.

Sample Poem

There was a young woman of York,
With a very strange fondness for pork.
Though it was far too big,
She ate the whole pig,
Without even using a fork!

A teacher, who tired of screaming
Came into class one day beaming.
"With my new walkman on,
Other noises are gone
and the scene that I see seems like dreaming!"

Bibliography

Children's Anthologies

Blishen, Edward, ed. *Oxford Book of Poetry for Children*. Oxford: Oxford University Press, 1963 (1986 edition).

Cole, William, ed. *Poem Stew*. New York: J.B. Lippincott, 1980.

Gensler, Kinereth and Nine Nyhart. *The Poetry Connection: An Anthology of Contemporary Poems with Ideas to Stimulate Children's Writing*. New York: Teachers and Writers Collaborative.

Hopkins, L. and M. Arenstein. *Time to Shout*. New York: Scholastic Book Services, 1972.

Koch, Kenneth and Kate Farrell, *Talking to the Sun*. New York: Henry Holt and Co., 1985.

Larrick, Nancy, ed. *Crazy to Be Alive in Such a Strange World*. New York: M. Evans Company, 1971.

Stevenson, Robert Louis. *A Child's Garden of Verses*. New York: Charles Scribners Sons, 1919.

Books About Teaching Poetry to Children

Greenberg, David. *Teaching Poetry to Children*. Portland, Oregon: Continuing Education Publications, 1985.

Kennedy, X.J. and Dorothy Kennedy. *Knock at a Star*. Boston: Little, Brown and Company, 1982.

Koch, Kenneth. *Wishes, Lies and Dreams*. New York: Harper and Row, 1970.

California Poets in the Schools Anthologies

These anthologies are extremely helpful in that they contain the best of student poetry for all grade levels as well as poetry from poet-teachers and articles by poet-teachers on instructional ideas and techniques they have found effective. The books also contain references for teachers and often fairly extensive bibliographies. These bibliographies can be ordered from California Poets in the Schools, 2845 24th St., San Francisco, California, 94110.

1980	*Easy Thing for You to Say*
1981	*My Eyes All Out of Breath*
1982	*All of a Sudden I Am One of Them*
1983	*Two Hearts the Color of Flesh*
1984	*This Poem Knows You*
1985	*Forgotten Languages*
1986	*Under the Bridge of Silence*
1987	*Thread Winding in the Loom*
1988	*True Wonders*

California Heritage Poetry Curriculum Collections

These books contain poems written by students who participated in the cross-curriculum project linking social studies and science with poetry under the auspices of the Oakland Unified School District. They also contain ideas that set up the poem writing exercises. Most ideas are for upper primary grades, but some ideas can be adapted for younger children. For information about these publications, contact the Oakland Unified School District, 1025 Second St., Oakland, CA 94606

1982-3	*Bay Leaf and Fool's Gold*
1983-4	*Califia's Children*
1984-5	*Dancing on the Brink of the World*
1985-6	*It Begins with Me*
1986-7	*Un techo del tamano del mundo* (bilingual Spanish curriculum)
	(A Roof the Size of the World)
1986-7	*Before and After My Cry* (Asian Curriculum)

Other References

Bierhorst, John, ed. *The Sacred Path: Spells, Prayers and Power Songs of the American Indians*. New York: William Morrow, 1983.

Gold, Lillian. *The Elementary School Publishing Center*. Bloomington: Phi Delta Kappa Fastback, 1989.

Momaday, N. Scott. *The Gourd Dancer*. New York: Harper and Row, 1976.

Niatum, Duane, ed. *Carriers of the Dream Wheel, Contemporary Native American Poetry*. New York: Harper and Row, 1975.

Roethke, Theodore. *Collected Poems*. New York: Anchor Books, 1975.

Credits

Lessons

Following are sources for ideas for some of the lessons presented in this book.

Lesson	Source
Doodle Poems	David Greenberg *
Spring Collage	Veronica Cunningham (CPITS)
Wish Poems	Kenneth Koch *
Noise Poems	Kenneth Koch and David Greenberg *
"I Know" Poems	David Greenberg *
Mask Poems	Jane Elsdon (CPITS) and *Califia's Children* *
Songs Our Names Sing	Devorah Major (*Two Hearts the Color of Flesh*) *
Animal Dreams	*David Greenberg* *

* Complete reference given in bibliography.

All other lessons were created by Lani Steele.

Poems

All uncredited poems were written by Lani Steele.

Poems by children were created in the following schools in the San Luis Coastal School District:
Sunnyside School
Baywood School
Teach School
Bellevue School
Hawthorne School